# Walking the Bricks

## Listening to the Soles of Your Feet

b. burk

# Walking the Bricks

## The Ramblings of a Man, His Dog, and His Camera

## b. burk

Railroad Street Press
St. Johnsbury, VT

Photographs by b. burk

LIBRARY OF CONGRESS

CATALOGING-IN-PUBLICATION DATA

---

Walking the Bricks / b. burk

First Printing

1 2 3 4 5 6 7 8 9 10

ISBN 978-1-936711-41-3

Railroad Street Press
394 Railroad St., Suite 2
St. Johnsbury, VT 05819

To my grandchildren and all their dreams

Jonathan

Benjamin

Owen

Samantha

Ethan

*Lunar eclipses 10-8-14 5:15am*

We miss the ordinary

Are surprised with the extraordinary

Overlook the present

Forget the past

Beg for the future

Run all day

And get nowhere

# Table of Contents

# Introduction

Buster and I started writing " Walk Abouts" in January of 2014. The fact is it was six degrees outside, Buster, the Beagle would not go out, the battery in my camera was too cold, and I was questioning how I could get more pictures published in the *New Castle Weekly*. Why not write a short, good feeling article and send it in to Mimi and Earl Carpenter, the paper's owners? They printed the article, along with a photograph. That is almost how it started. Writing would be the last suggestion anyone that knows me would make. It turns out I needed multiple editors. Eileen, my wife, a retired high school English teacher, Irene, a retired judge, Dan, a still active philosopher, and Buster, my faithful Beagle and companion all provided support

I keep a list of possible subjects, while current events increase the length of the list. I often use subject matter found in the Letters to the Editor, but with kindness and without name calling. If you anger people, they will never consider your ideas, and suggesting ideas to the town leaders are more palpable naked of any nastiness. An example of fodder from these letters was to have a dog yard, where dogs could run without a leash. See there may be more dogs in town than people. Another suggestion was to increase town parking. No changes in parking have been made in twenty years, while the visitors have increased.

Another goal of the" Walk About" is to have a smile or laugh; life is just too hard these days to keep the twine together. It always wants to unravel. So put your feet up, and laugh. If the laughter is at me or about me, that's great! The final goal of the "Walk About" has been to promote walking, or riding one's bike. We were never made to be a sedimentary animal. It is amazing what a little exercise will do to improve one's health.

Lastly don't forget the pictures. They speak louder and say more than any words I could ever write. People enjoy seeing something they are familiar with in the paper, even if it is a picture of themselves.

This book is a compilation of several "Walk Abouts", along with a multitude of local photographs, some previously published, but many newly released.

*New Castle is a destination. Many of those that have grown up here don't understand the treasures they have. From the old blue mailbox, to the churches established in 1589 and 1657, this village is surrounded by urbanization, while within our brick walkways and buildings one can hear the spirit of William Penn talking to the spirit of George Reed.*

*The simple fact that the first "Walk About" is titled Six Degrees (a very rare temperature in New Castle), tells the tale that this village is a very rare place. It is a living museum, as we hold on to our past, while we try to live in the present. We want our cell phones, but not the towers. We love our Delaware River, but fear pollution. There is not room in New Castle for everyone that wants to believe that Charles Dickens could have lived next door. But there is room in this world for everyone to take a little bit of New Castle home with them, and make the world a better place. Here we know that doing right is a struggle. We know you have to remain focused and vigilant. We know if we don't work hard, time will bury all that we are and we will disappear. So, welcome to New Castle and Six Degrees. May there always be a stove to warm your heart, soul, and feet.*

## Walk About

## Six Degrees

My usual daily trek to catch the sunrise starts a little before seven. This morning's sunrise is at 7:19am. Buster elects to stay in bed, as I swing my camera round my neck and set out into six degrees. New Castle is very quiet even for this rather late time. Windshield wipers are standing up as sentinels, watching and waiting for the enemy. He came last night as the sky's dandruff, while the polar express whistled in this chilling temperature, all done very quietly, while we were under our pile of covers.

I head for Bull Hill, a good location to capture sunrise. It's safer to walk in the road this morning than on the snow covered bricks. I'm thinking the village should be named Sleepy Hollow instead of New Castle. The only sound is from my L. L. Bean boots, a squeaky groan with each step. When I get to the park, I am stopped by the construction equipment, snow, and temporary fences, so I turn and head toward the Banks Building, still aware of the stillness all around me. Thinking it's amazing what six degrees can do to people, still under the covers, an extra tea or coffee, or a long look out the window. I start to think about 150 years ago, how did they do it? All huddled around the kitchen stove with an extra piece of coal, warming their hands, knowing they may never really be warm all day.

I turn onto Delaware Street from Second. I notice the grave of the tree that lived in front of Cloud Row. I turn and look back toward Delaware and East Third and think of that tree that was also removed. On toward the Banks building and another tree glides into my thoughts: the one that stood guard over the wharf for all those years. And then the tree along the *alleyway* between the Presbyterian Church and The Strand is missing. These mighty keepers of time were all young 150 years ago. They would know what was going on in New Castle's kitchens back then, and now they are only in our mind's eye. With modern equipment there is no evidence they even existed.

It's so cold on this morning even the coffee mug club is absent from the bench that was shaded by the old park tree. I turn and head back up Delaware and notice *The New Castle Weekly* is closed tight. Earl must be having an extra cup himself. I might as well do the same, as the battery in my camera gives up the ghost and says no more.

*New Castle Presbyterian Church*

*In the beginning, getting a weekly article published was not always clear sailing. Sometimes I would send in a "Walk About" and it was not used. Other times, I avoided sending one in because I could not take another rejection. The communication sidewalk between me and the New Castle Weekly was like a sidewalk missing a section or two. This was a time when I was trying to break into the newspaper business and Mimi and Earl were withdrawing.*

*The "Eagles" did make it to print. Most Americans, at least presently, have a soft spot for eagles.  Benjamin Franklin did not feel so inclined. I believe he favored the wild turkey for the national bird. DDT almost put an end to the mighty eagle. Those of us who spy on them know they will eat almost anything, but once in the air, they draw attention with their majestic flight. This "Walk About" also is the first of many that focuses on development.*

# Walk About

## Eagles

Sunrise was nine minutes earlier this day than last week, plus it's warmer and not snowing. It is now early afternoon, Buster and I head for Bull Hill for our after lunch walk. The snow has shrunk, the sun is bright, and the wind absent. The work on all the dykes has come to a standstill. As we get older and wiser we understand that we have no influence over Father Time, and Mother Nature. With all the advancements in our modern world, we have no control over Mother Nature's weather. I often think that the most recited prayer is, "Please don't rain on my parade, wedding, 4th of July, party..." Thus the work on the dykes is halted.

The dyke at Bull Hill is now naked, all the trees and brush have been removed and a new, improved, higher dyke in being placed along the Delaware River. I think back to the letters in *New Castle Weekly* a season or so back. One side wanted the trees and brush cut back to improve the view of our river. The other side was strongly against such removal and cited the needs of our wild life and advocated everything should be left alone.

Then super storm Sandy came ashore. The Army Corps of Engineers came to town and said that roots weaken dykes and the trees and brush must go. It appears they have the louder voice, and bigger stick, and the project money. The new appearance of Bull Hill will take a little getting used to, especially as it was overgrown and now it's not.

I came this way for the day before I saw a hawk in the marsh and was hoping to take a picture of one in flight. I was not disappointed. Within a minute, one went swiftly by, about six feet above the ground. Then I noticed a second hawk. Buster curled up on a pile of wood chips, nap time, while I sat with my camera posed. I was so focused on the hawks I did not notice that there were three mature eagles in an Oak tree. I re-directed my efforts. Within five minutes I was looking at seven mature bald headed eagles, one immature eagle (floating down the river on a chunk of ice), and two hawks.

Rachel Carson's, 1962, book, Silent Spring, focused on our need to protect nature. Since that point we have been improving, but for some, too slowly, for others, too quickly. Prior to the banning of DDT, the birds of prey were greatly reduced due to its deadly side effects. Eagles were placed on the endangered species list and protected. Now I am sitting watching eight eagles at one time. Never in my life did I ever imagine I would have such a moment.

Then I have this thought: are they here because the trees and brush has been removed? It is a frequent path I take and this is a very new sighting. Several of the eagles are perched in a large Oak tree, where they could see both, the river and the marsh, their sources for food. Last season they did not have the clear view and their flight path was disrupted. I am sure if the food supply lessens they will move to a tastier area. After I take several pictures and Buster wakes from his nap, we continue our walk about. I encourage you to walk, for each street, alley, and dyke in New Castle has a surprise to enjoy.

*Old ferry wharf, end of Chestnut*

*At the same time Buster and I were taking a serious look at New Castle and how it represented the past, the town hired Daniel Tjaden as our new Chief of Police. He moved up the river ten miles from Delaware City, and we moved down from Vermont, 448 miles. It was the little things Buster and I noticed that made us take pause. As he lifted his leg, I lifted my camera. This time it was at the blue mail box that still receives mail on the corner of East 2nd Street and Delaware Street. Chief Tijaden had a lot more to observe than an old Beagle and a babbling fool.*

# Walk About

## The Old Blue Mailbox

Buster and I are very new to New Castle when one hears about families that have lived in our village eight generations and have deeds that go back to the seventeen hundreds. I clearly remember my first walk about in New Castle. It was 2011 and how astonished I felt walking the streets. I was too overwhelmed to use my camera that was hanging around my neck. Clearly I was walking back in time – way back in time. George Reed lived here, and in fact, was laid to rest here. WOW!

The day after my first tour with Irene and Dan, while still wrapping my mind around Packet Alley, which referenced Crockett, Webster, and Jackson, Buster and I took an early morning walk. We started east on South Street and turned onto West 4th Street. Each house was an amazing discovery for me. Each tree was a special moment for Buster. We crossed Delaware and took a long look at the fountain. Perhaps that was my first picture taken in New Castle. Like any tourist, I stopped at the Court House, finally figured out that the Sheriff's building was "attached but separate", a phenomena that is very common in New Castle. I am not sure how many visits it took before I understood the street made of cobble stones, (Market Street) was different than East Second Street and my question was: whatever happened to the street that used to go through the building, now the town hall? Looking at Market Street I determined it was the longest

14

speed bump I had ever seen. When I saw my first car attempt Market Street, I sat on the bench next to the Arsenal and had a good laugh, and when they passed, they smiled and waved. From the town hall I crossed East Second and took the sidewalk back toward Delaware Street. I stopped at the gift shop, Cobblestone Gifts and realized where its name generated from. I took a couple of pictures of the courthouse and then stopped and stared at the blue box set atop a post: a mail box. In my mind I was thinking it was part of the history of the village and really not usable for mail. I touched it and found the little door actually opened. Buster left his mark and I took a picture. Like all the walkers, I headed for the river. I had my first look at the Banks Building and noticed it needed some repair. I noticed several cars came down Delaware Street, drove around the Bank's loop and back up Delaware. Funny, I found myself doing the same, only on foot.

Back at the mailbox, I took another picture and walked down to Sixth Street. During this time I finally absorbed how many bricks are in New Castle. My calculation came up with an answer of, "a lot". I once wrote we could call our village, Sleepy Hollow, but considering all the bricks, how about Brickville?

But back having a cup of tea, I could not get out of my mind the image of the blue mailbox atop the pedestal. Finally I walked back to the post office and asked the question, "Is the mailbox over there on East Second Street in use?" The postal clerk had an inquisitive look of "where did this one come from?" and replied, "Yes it works. Just pull down on the door and put your letter inside." I then asked, "And you will pick it up?" She assured me that in fact everyday it is opened and the mail is brought to the post office.

I had more questions for the postal clerk, but the line was building so I left. The next day I wrote to my five grandchildren and mailed the notes from the blue mailbox on the corner of East Second Street.

It's not that we have one of the last pedestal mailboxes left in the country, it's what this mail depository represents. For those who lived here for generations, it's a familiar part of our quaint village. For me, I marvel that this box survived post office cutbacks, disrespect by those with spray cans of paint, and foul objects placed inside. How did it live through all those too cold snowy winters, and more so, too hot summers?

I feel the old blue mailbox represents the uniqueness of historic New Castle. It is the result of the respect we have for each other and those who have gone before. New Castle lives on and on, remaining the same, while changing to remain the same. William Penn would feel as comfortable today as he did when he first stepped off the Delaware River onto Delaware Street.

*East Second Street & Delaware*

*You know the expression, "If I had a nickel for every time…"
This applies to the number of times I have spoken to a visitor,
seeing New Castle for the first time. Walking down the bricks,
people passing always express a greeting. Once they pass, the
visitor will undoubtedly ask me, "Do you know them?" The
reply is usually, " No", it's just what we do here in New
Castle." Heads shake and then they try it . They smile. They
are thinking, "I can't believe this! People actually say, " Hi"
around here."*

*When I was first exposed to this unique ritual, it made me
think of Madeline. This is way back in the old days, the
seventies, when companies had a greeter at the door, who
usually operated the switch board. You know if you were born
before 1985, when real people answered the phone. That tells
the story of New Castle. It's full of real people.*

*Delaware & Market Streets 2014*

# Walk About

# Madeline

This morning the sunrise was 6:45am with the sun warming New Castle for eleven hours and two minutes. I have already been to the river to look across to New Jersey, as the sun became visible. Now turning onto East Fourth Street, I always look at the corner house, across from the Amstel House. How tall it is, and thinking I wouldn't want to clean the leaves out of those gutters. The house continues on East Fourth Street. It appears to me that the brick garage belongs to the corner house. It doesn't appear the house is occupied. I wonder if the owner is aware of the aging process of the garage's roof? We all sag a little with age.

I continue on, Fourth Street, as all the streets in New Castle, have their own identiity. I enjoy the alleyway from East Fourth to East Third and find myself looking at the town Green, once a busy market place.

It's warm enough that I take advantage of one of the benches and Buster scours the Green for a squirrel to intimidate. He has never caught a squirrel, but he never gives up trying.

I think back to the phone call I made the night before. I had a computer question and called the toll free help number. We all know the routine: first the music, then just before I hang up a recorded voice states, "You are a valued customer. Please hold and the next available representative will assist you." More music, then a repeat of the recorded voice. My blood pressure climbs. I look at the computer trying to solve the issue myself, no luck. Finally a real person asks how they could help me. Yes, they must be speaking English, but no matter how much I work at understanding him, I fail. Now I have two failures, I can't get the computer program to do what I think it should be doing and I can't even understand an English speaking person, who says they want to help me. I say good night and hang up. Hours later I solve my issue and wonder if the programmer ever really used the program on a practical level.

While enjoying the morning watching New Castle wake up, with more people starting to walk their dogs, I think of Madeline. Thirty five years ago I worked for a company in Connecticut. I worked for this company for nine years and I believe there were two hundred people employed. I remember few of the people, except Madeline. Perhaps she was fifty and I was twenty-four when I started. Madeline was the company receptionist. She sat in a little glass booth at the front door and greeted people, mostly sales reps, as they walked in. She also answered the phone, "Good Morning, company name, how may I help you?" And suddenly, Madeline was your friend. Suddenly the person standing in front of her or on the phone had a smile and the moment was a good one. How did she do this? Madeline was perfectly matched for the position. It was a long walk from where Madeline worked her magic and I took up space, but it was a worthwhile detour to walk out and say good morning to her, and I always felt better when I did take the trip.

On Friday afternoon, one would think it would be a slow time for Madeline, weekend bound, but no, customers called to wish her a good weekend. In reality they just wanted to hear her wish them a good weekend. The Christmas cards she received covered the walls of the lobby. The president of the company said she was the best salesperson we had.

When I walk on the dyke past the saling club, many a morning I pass a woman who has a "Madeline" voice and when she says her good morning to me, I smile and think of the Madeline past. Where are all the Madelines? We believe we can't afford the "Madelines" anymore, but in reality we can't afford not to have them. They made us feel the joy of life that the grunge of the day often buried.

I should return to the kitchen table for morning tea but it's just too nice. Buster is content and I continue to mind wander. What if we had a few greeters that walked around in period clothing and greeted visitors and welcomed them to historic New Castle? The Chamber of Commerce must know what days are the busiest. They must know how many people want New Castle to be a destination location, or on the other hand, want our town to be a quiet hamlet. Regardless, New Castle, good morning, have a good day and a fine walk.

*Immanuel Church on the Green*

*The process of setting up residence in New Castle was a slow one. Eileen and I moved on New Castle time. We used the trustee's time piece. Most feel it stopped about one hundred, fifty years ago. Buster wanted to know what was taking so long. There are enough trees here, let's get the tail on! First we rented on East Second Street. That was a very good time. We enjoyed it very much. Pam and Victor were wonderful hosts. It was a time of exploring, meeting people, and making sure New Castle was ready for us.*

# Walk About

## Buster Decides to Stay

Dear reader, by the time you get to read this Walk About it will be March! The weekend past we had some warm weather, just a tease my neighbor warned; the gulls were flying and the geese were dancing. The villagers was walking, smiling, and greeting each other. Some were cleaning up, others doing repairs, items that were bugging them. Regardless, everyone was smiling. There were basketballs bouncing in Battery Park, a kite was dipping and spinning, the tennis courts were humming, and I even saw a set of golf clubs marching down Harmony Street. And if that is not enough good news, the snow melted, and ran down the drain. What a few degrees in temperature will do for our dispositions.

But what was brought to my attention was that I did not finish our arrival story to New Castle, mentioned in my blue mailbox article. The continued story starts and finishes with the real estate agencies that put those fliers in front of homes that are for sale. So it's their fault. In these times we seem to blame others and not take responsibility for our actions, so why not blame them? Or should I thank them?

On our second visit to New Castle, while Buster and I were walking about, he would bless a tree and I would pick up a sales flyer. At this moment Buster and I decided we should buy a house and become residents of New Castle.

With our fliers in hand, Buster ready for a nap, we returned to our host home on Sixth Street and I announced, "Eileen we should buy a house in New Castle." Since I was full of excitement, it appears I missed a few words and reactions that took place. It is reported to me as follows: it seems two people may have fallen to the floor. I really believe that they put their heads down and left the room. Eileen had a few words for me to chew on. Actually they were a series of questions: Are you serious? Have you gone over the edge? Is your light bulb on? What's in the water? What will the kids say? What I remember her saying was, "O.K. Dear. We will have to investigate your idea," which I interpreted as, "YES."

It was agreed the four of us would take a walk gathering more fliers - down Sixth, up Fifth, across Chestnut, down, up, down, and back to South Street. Even Buster was tired when we returned to West Sixth Street. I spread all the fliers across the dining room table. It was more fun than looking at the spring seed catalogs. With so many choices, it was finally decided that we should rent an apartment and determine if New Castle and Buster were a good match. Eileen is so reasonable! We left the next morning for a month's stay at Carolina Beach, NC, while Irene agreed to scout out some apartments.

Within a few days we received an email from Irene that she had the perfect place for us on East Third Street. Attached were some wonderful photographs... well almost. It appeared that Irene was taken by the crown molding in the apartment and that is all we saw. Based on her recommendation and a phone conversation with the owner, we had an apartment on East Third Street for the next year.

Pam, the owner, was a wonderful help and town representative. Buster loved the fenced -in side yard and Pam's hanging of seasonal decorations from her weeping cherry tree increased my smile. Now you know how we started our adventures and love affair with New Castle. The people we meet always have suggestions for a new activity, a new trek, a longer bike ride, or a quiet place to enjoy conversation and a cup of tea. You still do not know how Buster ended up on Harmony Street and that will have to wait for another time. Have a good day, greet those you meet, and have a fine walk about.

*New Castle, Delaware is like every other town in the United States, and New Castle, Delaware is like no place you have every been. For many economic reasons, thank goodness, New Castle has been overlooked many times. Just two examples of this would be in 1879, New Castle lost the county court to Wilmington. The lawyers moved out of town. On August 15th 1951, the Delaware Memorial Bridge was opened. This meant the ferry service between New Castle, Delaware and Pennsville, New Jersey was now obsolete.Both towns lost a major source of income. Since I live on the west side of the river, I direct my thoughts to New Castle. On that lazy summer day, New Castle was forgotten. What was left were people who searched for a new direction. They found the past to be their future. What I found when I got here sixty plus years later was a village of very good people who decided to protect the past and welcome visitors, goodness, and the future.*

*In 2014, New Castle saw a change in newspaper ownership. Terry and Alice took over from Mimi and Earl, as owners and editors. This change was supported by the community, for our paper lived on. At the same time this town realized that not all people have the same level of respect for what we want to protect. Battery Park is a fine example of some sad practices. Regardless of the trashing of our park, the village as a whole will not stand for such behaviors. Citizens contine to write their letters to the editors of the New Castle Weekly, and support the dedicated work of the trustees to keep our town a beautiful and welcoming place.*

*Delaware River*

# Walk About

## We Are All in This Together

With the news over the past two weeks concerning the closing of the *New Castle Weekly*, I panicked. What will I do without my source of information regarding the village of New Castle? I know I always have the sidewalks for information. Yes, it's good stuff, but I must say that the *New Castle Weekly* brings credibility to all the waging tongues. I had a few sleepless nights. How will I know about the birds, and the days gone by? How will I know what the planning committee is planning? Will life go on? I need my supply of letters to the editor and those Walk Abouts are my best avenue for useless information.

It is always better to remain calm within the storm and ask oneself these three questions: first, "What is the worst thing that can happen?" Next, "What is the best thing that can happen?" and "What will probably happen?" We now know without missing a step, Mimi and Earl passed the baton and the *New Castle Weekly* continues to provide what we need to know.

Now to move on to an issue that continues to frustrate me to the point of boiling my blood pressure. That is the cleanliness of Battery Park. This walkable, playable, family gathering place is a treasure beyond words. Just a few weeks ago, more than seventy people gathered to pick up and remove the debris left over the cold winter months. The volunteers collected and removed tons of garbage. For a few short hours our park sparkled and then before you could count the geese in the park some people started dropping their litter, leaving their dog's waste, treating the park with disregard and disrespect. For the good of the order, we have a policy which states "What you bring in please take out." I would like to offer this guideline, "If you won't leave it in your own front yard, please don't leave it in our Battery Park."

Now before you say, there he goes again being the town crier with few facts to support his podium, you must know what goes on while most of us are still in bed. I know you are thinking, "I was just in the park for my walk and it looks clean to me. What is this old, babbling, dried up stream talking about? Let's have the padded wagon take him for a ride, or better yet, let's get a small boat and take him out to one of the ice breakers and leave him there. He can talk to the seagulls till his voice sinks into the west with the setting sun." I have to tell you about Lynn. She is a good person, who always has a smile and a "Good morning", plus a pail. I don't know how early she gets up but she beats me to the park most days. What does Lynn do you ask? Well she picks up after us, especially those who go to the park in the later hours and leave their trash behind. I have never heard Lynn complain. She just gets another pail, another plastic bag and cleans our Battery Park, so it sparkles each morning, so our visitors and we can enjoy another walk along the Delaware River. When you come across Lynn, please thank her, and when you come across one of the trustees, thank them for having the foresight to employ Lynn.

The dyke beyond the sailing club is finished with its new black top coating. Take a walk. It's beautiful. There are a few Wood Duck eggs at the corner of East Second Street and Harmony. Someone was kind and put a sign up to identify them. If anyone has time on their hands for the next twenty one days, please consider helping mother Wood Duck by sitting on the eggs. I will bring you some water and old sandwiches if I remember. I would also bring out some old, really old magazines, like the ones on the table of your dentist, for you to read. And finally let us all help Lynn whenever we can: carry it in, carry it out, watch the Delaware flow and have a pondering walk.

*The best thing that has happened to me was I have grown older. With that I have slowed down. Some due to the body moving slower, while another part of the reduced speed is I have learned to listen, feel, and observe better. Becoming part of New Castle is a fine example of this changed insight. It has taken Eileen, Buster and I three years to become members in this community. By taking an extended period to observe, taste, and search our "soles" we landed on Harmony Street. We have no regrets, only delights. We divide our time between Vermont and New Castle. We fine the joy of two worlds and are blessed to be lead to two locations we love to be part of. We thank Bob and Delores for Vermont and Irene and Dan for New Castle.*

31

# Walk About

## Harmony Street

I just took a look back on the past two "Walk Abouts". I sometimes take myself too seriously. It's good to have friends like Irene and Dan. The four of us take our afternoon constitutional, similar to British high tea. Dan and Irene would walk their dog, Joey, now deceased, while Eileen and I walked Buster, as arrogant as ever. Well, Irene mentioned last Tuesday that walking with us is better than having a dog. "How?", I asked. "You get Dan and me out of the house for our exercise, and we don't have to clean up after you."

I remember back when asked to babysit for Samantha, our granddaughter. Eileen and Jen wanted to go shopping. No problem. They were no sooner out the door when Sam asked if I wanted to have tea. "OK" I replied. Before the grass could grow I was wearing a lady's hat from the fifties and a pink boa. Every five year old girl has a pink boa in the closet for just such an occasion. I was not taking the tea very seriously, but then I noticed Samantha was. Boy did I drink a lot of warm water! Just this week Eileen asked me what I had planned for the day, and I replied, "Nothing". She commented that was what I did yesterday and I smiled and said, "And I didn't finish." We really should not take ourselves too seriously; it's most likely the root for high blood pressure, along with too much salt.

In other thoughts, John mentioned after reading about the town wish list that the reason all the service wires are underground on Delaware, Second, and Market Street is thanks to Oprah Winfrey and a movie she made. I suggest we invite her back and see what she can do with a few more of our historic streets and I hope the trustees have a plan to invite movie makers to New Castle. We are very unique. We have been here before the United States was here. That makes us keepers of history; no one is like us.

The construction companies are working full steam ahead, despite the weather on the dykes. They are bringing the projects up to final grade, where we will soon see the final layers put into place. The Broad dyke is receiving a serious makeover from top to bottom. The equipment is endless and the delivery of processed material continuous. Readers, soon we will be walking the dykes! Before I move on to how Buster got to Harmony Street, I noticed several trees came down this week. There were good reasons for their removal and remember there are better reasons for their replacement.

Now, for how Buster ended up living on Harmony Street… In the spring of 2012 we established ourselves on East Third Street. We would sit under the weeping Cherry Tree and enjoy the hanging Easter eggs, or Christmas décor. For whatever the season, Pam would direct Victor to place these eye catching, windblown, magical dancing items from the branches. Buster and I would take our daily Walk About. From the River up to Ferry Cutoff Street, up and down Chestnut Street we would tread. We would watch the tennis players on South Street and wonder who chases a ball more, a golfer or a tennis player? On a good day we would come home with a real estate flyer. On a great day we would arrange for a house tour and on a wonderful day Eileen would go with us for the viewing. Buster and I became accustom to Eileen's list of "Nos". She suffered from Goldilocks' syndrome: this house is too big, this one is too small, the stairs are too narrow, or the floors are not flat. But we would protest. These houses are hundreds of years old; one would have to expect some settling.

Then one day a for sale sign went up on Harmony Street. Eileen noticed it on Friday and she picked up the flyer. The flyer stated there would be an open house on Sunday at 1:00pm. Between church, a planned bike ride, and Eileen going to the opera, I did not pursue the open house. On Sunday noon when I mentioned I was off for a bike ride Eileen asked, "What about the open house?" Well the ears on Buster lifted and his eyes rolled and I stopped all movement. We were first in line when the door opened at 1:00pm. That is to say Eileen was first in line. Buster and I were behind. By the time she reached the dining room and Buster blessed the tree in the "grassless, hard-scaped" backyard, Eileen said, "Let's make an offer." That is the end of the story. Chris was a wonderful agent. Even when there was a glitch, it was resolved in no time, and we moved in late June of 2013. Buster found it to his liking, Eileen was always in love with the house and has enjoyed decorating, and I am still in the habit of picking up flyers.

And before I forget again there is a general clean up for Battery Park on Saturday, April 19th, starting at 9:00am. I hope you can join the fun. Have a great week, don't take life so seriously, and have a fine walk about.

*There are more forms of government and civic committees in New Castle than one can imagine. Or perhaps it just feels that way to me. Coming from northern Vermont where the word "government" is not allowed at the table, here, we are very open about our governing bodies. In fact the subject is well debated, and we are not short of experts. I enjoy the morning group that meets at the Banks Building. The subject of the day can be far and wide. But in the end, it comes down to money, and who will it help. Jim and Paul are as wise as they come. Jim walks regardless of weather and Paul does the same only on his bike. When they talk, I listen. And there are many people we should be listening to. Bill Ney the science guy says, "Everyone we met knows something we do not." Listening is a gift that provides a worthy education.*

*As you can see from the Walk Abouts, I don't take myself too seriously. My biggest job these days is fighting old age and I'm going to lose. That's the way of life, so treat it with kindness and you will be remembered that way.*

*Battery Park*

# Walk About

# Side by Each

At times dear readers you may detect some negativity in my thoughts but not today. Recently I attended a committee meeting and then I found myself at a council meeting. I just could not watch another Phillies' game after Sunday. New Castle is the luckiest place in the world. If you do not agree, I would suggest you move and see how life is in any other location and then you will dream of returning. Our town leadership is dedicated, composed of concerned men and women who give us hundreds of hours of their time and knowledge. On the record, thank you. And thanks to all of you who stop me on the sidewalk just to say "Hi". Thanks for not throwing an old tomato.

Perhaps a month ago I mentioned that the dyke beyond the sailing club was nearly finished, and I was looking forward to seeing both walkers and bikers using the path for exercise, conversation, and calorie removal. And if you remember, I was taken aback by comments regarding the walkers not liking the bikers and the bike users preferring the walkers build their own path.

Let me say just a few words about Jim and Paul. They are old friends, perhaps unlikely, with one being a biker and one a walker. Still they see eye to eye. Jim is a native to New Castle. He is retired; in his life, every day is a Saturday. Paul on the other hand is from Connecticut. He came to this area for college and never left. He still works as he is younger than Jim. He rides his bike year round, new dyke, old dyke, or no dyke. Get to the point, I can hear you yelling. O.K, O.K., but good points take a moment to develop.

In this Walk About, the picture tells the story. Jim and Paul are in conversation, while both using their own mode of transportation. A walker and a rider together, a tire and a shoe leather sharing the same path with respect for each other. Jim and Paul are two of the kindest, respectful, knowledgeable people I know. If you really want to know how New Castle was thirty, forty, or fifty years ago, ask Jim. If you want someone to listen to you and provide a second choice, just ask Paul. It is people like these two old friends that make New Castle work so well. They are who we are. They leave the park, or our streets and alleys the same way they find them, so the next person feels he/she is the first to step on that spot. And the good news is New Castle is full of people like Jim and Paul, Irene and Eileen, Terry and Alice, Jim and Bertie, Esther and Linda. The list is considerable!

I do have a concern, now that the first dyke is basically completed. It's wider, flatter, longer, and safer. What are we going to fret about? The dyke has been our focus for two years and longer. We feared it would not meet our expectations. Now, all we can do is smile and become one of the many who is now using its many healthy benefits. In hindsight, I am not sure I heard anyone say, "We just have to trust our trustees, council people, and citizen committees." I take my cap off to them. Well done "old friends". I see we are now turning our sights on the town's parking situation. It's only been in committee since 1995, and I am sure we will have a few letters to the editor starting, "I remember when we let the horses park on both sides of Market Street and they were allowed in the first floor of the town hall." I suggest we take our walk, sit on our porch, watch the Phillies and trust those with the talent to be keepers of New Castle.

Final words: Alice, how did you get a vacation with being on the job one week? Terry, I am sorry about the computer issue plaguing you as you try to get the New Castle Weekly out. Jim did you ever find your car? Please remember the pavement is getting hot and our dogs do not wear shoes. The mother Wood Duck is doing her thing, with one week down and two to go. Take a walk and see the world with a renewed view.

Separation Day

Buster has been my walking partner and inspiration for the "Walk Abouts". Four times a day he insists on a long walk so he can look for squirrels. In Vermont, he's free to roam and in New Castle he is leashed. He does not seem to mind the leash, *and in fact I believe he prefers New Castle. Buster is a strange dog. He has a mind of his own and an attitude to go along with his outlook. "Don't bother me, I'm hunting" or "Bruce, walk faster." His eyes could express his thoughts. And if does not get me moving, there is the barking and pulling on the leash.*

*Buster*

## Walk About

## Buster

I use to be the boss when no one was home. That was until Buster came to live with Eileen and me. Now my title is "housekeeper" when Buster and I hold down the fort. The last words I always hear as Eileen leaves are, "Please keep the house clean and stay off the internet; we don't need a thing!"

We have to go back about seven years. Eileen was traveling with Jennifer, our daughter, who does educational consulting. After a few days alone, I got a little squirrelly. I had done all the dishes, since I ran out. The house was clean, as I was looking for my sneakers. I decided to watch the News on television. There was a segment on a local organization that rescued dogs and placed them for adoption with qualified families. It had been many years since "Bear", our Elkhound, passed. I walked over to the computer and sent out an email stating, "We are a qualified family." In return I received a thirteen page application. Having time on my hands, I filled out the form and sent it back. The following morning I had a return email, "Yes, we qualified." With a few more exchanges, an appointment was made to go to the shelter and see a Bulldog/Boxer mix. A few minutes later Eileen called and asked if anything was new. Apparently I failed to mention the rescue dog idea.

Eileen returned from her trip. She was very impressed with the clean house, and my "to do list" that was up to date. Some chores on the list were years old. Next we had a spirited conversation about adopting a dog. These spirits were not the angel type! I was reminded of the old adage, "Life begins when the kids move out and the dog dies." The question was put on the table, "Why ruin a good thing?" The compromise reached was to at least look at the dog.

When we arrived at the rescue center we were told that the Bulldog/Boxer mix had been adopted, but they had a nice little Beagle. Eileen was quick to say, "Let's go," but this cute little dog, with big eyes, was looking up at us. Before you could say "Harmony Street" we were on the floor and Buster was showing his good side. We decided to take this 11 inch Beagle home and give him a three week try, referred to as an adjustment period.

I then noticed a woman and three children sitting in the far corner of the room. When Eileen and I said Yes", on cue the family started crying. It was explained to us that the children were home schooled and as a school project they were a foster family for dogs waiting to be adopted. Apparently Buster was with them longer than normal (more than six months), as he was returned several times from his adjustment trials. This should have been clue number one!

After passing the tissue box around and hugging and promising the exchange of pictures, Buster and all his belongings were placed in our car. Buster immediately curled up and went to sleep. In our conversation home we decided this was going to be easy. To this day Buster is happiest in a car.

When we pulled into the driveway, the newest member of our family was still sleeping. I opened the car door and like lightning Buster was out of the car and gone. Five hours later I found Buster or perhaps he found me. I immediately put the leash to him and we had a conversation about the rules and which one of us was the boss. Well, Eileen and I live in a post and beam house in Vermont and when Buster reached the first post he lifted his leg. I guess to tell both of us who was the boss.

Reader, I am out of space. There is so much more to tell you about Buster. Till then, I leave you with this thought: I have met many people that have owned a beagle, but none that have owned two. Keep walking, and if you see a beagle, keep going.

*We come to the moment that I did not believe would happen this year. Many unexpected events take place in a year. Sometimes one can't wait for New Year's Eve and all the opportunities. We are basically optimists and that is good. That is how we make it day to day. The sun will be bright and the day richer. That is how Buster faced each morning. It was a new opportunity to catch a squirrel. He never did in his nine years, but he never gave up. I don't know if it was this enthusiasm, or the fact that Buster was fiercely independent that resulted in my liking him so much. It just seemed he was always there at my side and when he was not, the sadness and loneliness was more than I ever expected. He and I had plans for our first anniversary of writing the" Walk About". Now I tear up when I look at his picture, that sits on my desk. Dear friends, I hope that at least once you have the treasure of having a pet that is a true companion.*

## Walk About

## Buster the Beagle

Kind reader, there are a few more "tails" to tell about Buster. I have written about him many times in the past, but unexpectedly this is the time to put pen to paper. As you know Buster was a rescue dog. He came with a sordid past, including physical abuse. It took a few years before we knew the entire story of Buster's life prior to his adoption.

The first Buster event happened when Eileen, Buster, and I were walking on the beach in South Carolina. He was on his leash and I stopped to talk with a gentleman who was seated in a low beach chair. You know the type of chair, the one with practically no legs. While talking about fishing, Buster went over to the chair and lifted his rear leg. What could I say but, "Have a nice day."

When we received Buster, he suffered greatly from separation anxiety. We could not leave him and if we did, we learned quickly that there would be damage done. We worked with Dr. Jill, Buster's veterinarian and slowly we could leave him for a minute, then five minutes. We worked up to thirty minutes. On a hot summer day in Vermont, we needed to go to town and decided to leave Buster in the house. Our trip took a little longer than expected, but when we returned the house was in perfect condition. We showered Buster with treats and praise. That evening, when I went to the bedroom to put my tired feet in my slippers, I found them filled with #2!

The last "tail" to record took place last year when Immanuel Church had their blessing of the animals. I took Buster, thinking he needed all the help he could get. Eileen would have no part of this decision, so Buster and I wandered over and took a pew. When it was our turn, Father Keene blessed Buster with holy water and Buster blessed the Church with his water. Taking Buster home, I quickly returned with cleaning products.

From time to time, Buster would come up lame and have difficulty walking. We discovered with the help of Dr. Jill that he had a degenerative spinal condition that was not uncommon among Beagles, but was exacerbated in Buster, as the X-rays showed he had several bird shot pellets in his body, some in areas that were potentially dangerous. When his back went out, he would be back to normal in a week, with medication and rest. However, we were warned that this condition would worsen in time, and he was not a candidate for surgery. I believe his back went out four times prior to last week. All summer, Buster was himself, chasing squirrels and jumping rock walls. In all of his 8 years, he never caught a squirrel, but he never gave up hope. Then, while playing on Thursday, Buster stopped. He was paralyzed. All the king's men could not put him back together again.

Buster loved New Castle. Being from Tennessee, he damned the cold, Vermont winters and much preferred the moderate snows of Delaware. He always wanted to die here, but last week we were in Vermont avoiding the mid-Atlantic heat when he passed.

New Castle is down a couple of Beagles. His best, Beagle friend, Frankie, who lived on West 3rd recently moved and now Buster is in greener pastures. When you walk today, seek the face of a four legged friend. Look at it kindly, and take your smile back and wear it so the next person you meet will smile. You never know how that smile might brighten the day of others.


*This "tale" of Buster has been told a thousand ways over a thousand years. Think outside the box. It is easy to see the ones that do and the ones that do not. The retail stores that were so important when I was a kid and now are gone. Buster's box was different than my box. He taught me to be open minded. Standing still is not the same as taking a rest. We can't stand still or we would still all have an outhouse and chickens in the back yard. But it appears to me we still need to learn how to take a rest. We still need to learn that we are different from each other and that's wonderful. We still need to learn there is more peace in breaking bread together than throwing stones at each other.*

*New Castle from the east end of Delaware Street, 2014*

# Walk About

## Conundrum

With Buster on my mind, I have been stewing in a conundrum recently. It was a long running one. But I have developed a theory on how Buster was aware of his surroundings. Yes, I still need to mention Buster now and then, for in many ways he was an enigma. After reading my solution you just may say, "What took you so long to figure that out?" Conundrum, conundrum, conundrum besides being an exciting word to say ten times fast, a conundrum is a good thing to have, as it makes us think outside our comfort zone, wake up some gray cells that have been sleeping too long, and lets our mothers call us "sunny.'

Now back to Buster, the Beagle. Beagles have a reputation for a few distinguishing features. They are ornery, have an exceptionally good sense of smell, and are on the low end of the list for brain capacity. With that said, reader, Buster loved to take a car ride. He had his pink and turquoise, polyester, crocheted afghan - a Christmas present that Buster pulled out of the closet and claimed as his. The blanket stayed in the car on the floor behind the driver's seat. He would burrow into the polyester for each trip and then about a minute before we arrived he would jump up on the seat and be ready for action. The conundrum was, "How did Buster know we had arrived at our destination?" Whether it be our summer home in Vermont, our children's homes in Maine, or Harmony

Street, Buster somehow knew when we arrived before the car stopped.

Eileen and I would have our usual conversation pondering this phenomenon. Could he sense our excitement? Did he remember the bumps in the road? He can't tell time, or read the GPS, could he? See we all try to solve a problem or conundrum from our point of view, using our strongest senses and experiences. The problem was, I was not thinking from Buster's strongest sense, and like most people I don't know how to walk, only run, shutting out all the beauty around me. I walk with a purpose instead of walking without a purpose, a time table, or thinking about what I want to do next. This running life style is why we don't sleep well at night, don't listen to others, and even more concerning, don't take the time to understand each other's point of view and destination.

Allow me an example from Buster's point of view – his nose. How many times when you walk into someone's home, you realize the home has a distinctive fragrance? It may be pleasant or not. Every living entity has its own fragrance and as runners we miss most of this except at night when I walk Market Street and the smell of garlic comes wafting up from Delaware Street.

New Castle has a scent and Buster could smell it when he arrived in town, while most of us miss it unless it is very strong and usually unpleasant. We as humans think we are stronger in every way over other animals and this is not true. Have you ever seen a butterfly and a bumble bee enjoying nectar from the same flower, if not you need to re-learn to walk and take a deep breath. Buster could smell the bricks of New Castle, along with the sycamores, roses, grass, and Delaware River. Beyond the physical smells, I am sure he could smell the positive outlooks, the residents of New Castle radiate. This is the reason Buster loved New Castle and our many visitors do the same.

The mystery of how Buster knew he was in New Castle is solved in my mind. Now, on to the next conundrum. This week, leave the cell phone on the counter, the watch next to the sink, and take a walk to nowhere, with no particular destination in mind, here in New Castle. Take a walk, take a deep breath, and smell the bricks.

*It was difficult for me to pick the "Walk Abouts" for this book. I am not sure if it means that I liked them all a little too much, or none of them enough. The goal for all of them has been the same. Point out something to think about, have a little laugh at me or Buster, get out and exercise, for the older you are the more important this is, and enjoy a picture of God's creation.*

*Below is the last "Walk About" for this book. It was printed in the New Castle Weekly just before Thanksgiving of 2014. Here in our country we have officially entered the Holiday season, first, to thank our maker for another year of harvest, and next, to ask our maker for joy and peace worldwide. We end our holiday season with New Year's Eve, entering winter, but we carry our life experiences of joy, hope, and blessings forward into the new year.*

*This is a Thanksgiving story, a very true one. It took place in 1958. I was ten years old, too young to know much that was not in black or white, and old enough to know there was stuff going around me that I didn't understand. And when I asked, I was told, "Not to worry about it.  You won't understand."  Or, "You shouldn't be listening to the adults." The reason I like this story so much is it could have been painted by Norman Rockwell and ended up as the cover of Saturday Evening Post. This is significant for me because there were few such events in my young life.*

*For this season of joy and hope, I pray that each one of you has at least one story that you like to linger over, like a good cup of Earl Gray, or a glass of your favorite brandy. And I hope you have someone who will sit and listen to you retell the story, year after year. Even if it is a community of one, it's better than being alone. So here is my Thanksgiving story, my gift to you.*

## Walk About

## Emil's Thanksgiving Turkey

Dear reader, as we enter our season of hope and pardon, permit me to wish you all your dreams come true between now and New Year's Eve. Then, we all know, we enter winter, the dark season, the hardest time to find joy and hope, with long, winter nights and short, windy, cold days. My feet will not be warm until April and all the brandy in New Castle County will not help that problem. Sit down with a cup of tea and enjoy this true story about one day in my childhood. It was 1958 and I was ten years old. The Burk clan was at my grandfather's retired farm on Notch Road, in Simsbury, Connecticut for Thanksgiving. Back then, that part of Connecticut was as rural as Vermont and as cold. Grandfather Emil was already sixty two and his heart was weak. This was the last year for this family gathering, for after that, Grandpa and Grandma went to Florida to avoid the cold winters.

The farmhouse was big, and very old, and very drafty, plus squeaky, especially the floors. The house was heated with the kitchen stove, which was a combination coal for heat and hot water, and propane for cooking. In the stone walled cellar was a large coal furnace, with one register directly above it that opened at the entrance to the bathroom, living room, and grandma's bedroom. The house was always too hot. The smell of coal was always present.

This Thanksgiving must have been a cold one, as the ground was covered with a hearty deep cushion of snow. So much snow was unusual for Connecticut, that early in the season. Inside the warm farmhouse were the usual suspects. There were fourteen grandchildren, four married couples, and two grandparents. When we were all together (just a few times a year, as my family lived some distance away), my grandfather was the happiest, my grandmother was most nervous, and the grandchildren were the craziest. The four married couples (our parents) argued from the first hello to the last goodbye. There were two sets of Republicans, and two sets of Democrats. Bless them all. I can hear them from heaven.

The kitchen was a large room, but a small space for gathering. It must have been thirty feet by thirty feet, but the coal stove took lots of room, plus the refrigerator. Then there was the ringer washing machine. There were no built-ins back then. There were four doors in the kitchen, and grandma's rocking chair. In the center of the room, was the old, farm, kitchen table, oil skin covered, and all set for the feast. The space that remained was a small walkway around the kitchen. It was time to eat. I am sure the turkey was over cooked, very dry, but golden brown. It always was. We focused on the golden brown.

Grandma was giving orders, at least shouting orders. The main table was set except for the turkey; it was still on the counter and would be carved at the table. There was a lot of talking, and then Grandma yelled to Emil, "Emil you fool. If you don't watch it, that damn turkey is going to end up on the floor." Twenty two of us turned to look at our grandpa and grandma just as the turkey slid from the platter and tried to escape by sliding toward the backyard door, the door that was only opened in the summer. What I remember the most was the silence. It seemed to last a very long time. Then grandpa walked over to the turkey, picked it up and placed it back on the platter. As he took a step toward the table, he said, "It's time to eat."

It was a very joy-filled and fun Thanksgiving. In fact it was the happiest I remember. The turkey was great. Grandma called Emil a fool a few more times, and he winked at his grandchildren. After dinner, we went out to the hayfield with the hill and went sledding. It was cold and getting dark. David was the oldest cousin. If I was ten, he could have been sixteen. He said it was time to go back to the farmhouse. We all walked back together talking about the day when David asked the question to the wind, "Do you think Grandpa dropped the turkey on purpose?" It was the second period of silence I experienced that day. And to this day, the question has never been answered. Dear readers, eat well, give thanks, and don't forget to walk.

# Final Thoughts

"It was the best of times, it was the worst of times, it was the age of wisdom, it was the age of foolishness … it was the spring of hope, it was the winter of despair, we had everything before us, we had nothing before us …"

Charles Dickens wrote these words in 1859. New Castle was already an old city. I read Dickens often and think about his words always. He points out the difference between being an optimist and a pessimist.

In this year, we live in a broken system. The federal government is at a standstill and is sinking in its own muck. State and local governments are somewhat more successful and are re-inventing themselves, after most of them have reached the edge of the abyss of financial disaster. For years the baby boomers were talked about as if they lived on another planet. Now that they are ready for retirement, the government wants to ship them to another planet. Baby boomers (self included) may just be a group of Americans that will see more discrimination, and neglect, than any other group.

We have to make our own fun, take care of each other in our own neighborhoods, knowing full well, that we live in Charles Dickens' times ("it was the best of times, it was the worst of times"). I leave you with this suggestion: be an optimist, exercise a lot, take your nap, speak out with respect, and remember you live in your time.

Finally a few more thanks to give... Bob, this book was your idea. I hope you enjoy it. To Earl and Mimi, who published my first "Walk About", thank you very much. Alice and Terry, you are the *New Castle Weekly*. We all thank you for putting out the best small town paper in the country. To my son, Christopher, who I once advised and who now advises me; it has been a good transition. Dan and Irene, thanks for inviting us to visit New Castle. I hope you don't regret we stayed.

To my best friend Eileen, I love you. You are the best editor, advisor, and companion one could pray for. And finally to Buster, we started the "Walk About" together. May you always chase squirrels and remember me fondly.

www.ingramcontent.com/pod-product-compliance
Lightning Source LLC
Chambersburg PA
CBHW042145170626
46815CB00006BA/318